The Bumper Book of ...

Christmas Songs

© 2001 by International Music Publications Ltd
First published by International Music Publications Ltd in 2001
International Music Publications Ltd is a Faber Music company
Bloomsbury House 74–77 Great Russell Street London WC1B 3DA

ISBN10: 0-571-52911-9
EAN13: 978-0-571-52911-7

Editor: Anna Joyce
Cover Design: IMP Studio
CD Production: Artemis Music Ltd
Cover Image: © Photodisc Inc 2001

Another Rock and Roll Christmas

Words and Music by
Mike Leander, Eddie Seago and Gary Glitter

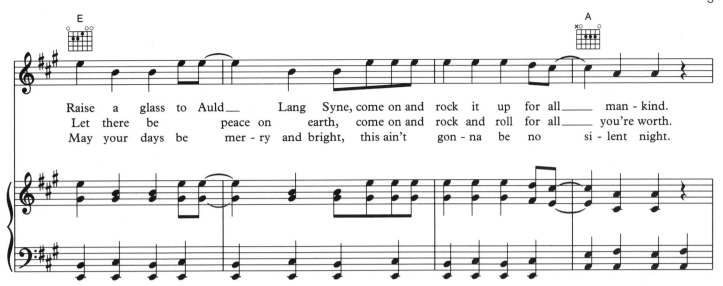

Raise a glass to Auld__ Lang Syne, come on and rock it up for all____ man - kind.
Let there be peace on earth, come on and rock and roll for all____ you're worth.
May your days be mer - ry and bright, this ain't gon - na be no si - lent night.

Good to see__ friends I know kiss-ing un - der the mis - tle - toe, I
We're gon - na laugh, we're gon - na sing, we're gon - na make the raft - ers ring,
See the stars__ glit - ter-ing,__ soon they're gon - na see the New Year in,

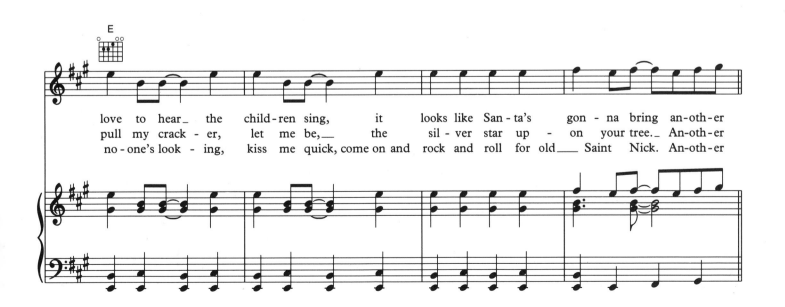

love to hear_ the child - ren sing, it looks like San - ta's gon - na bring an-oth-er
pull my crack - er, let me be,__ the sil - ver star up - on your tree. An - oth - er
no - one's look - ing, kiss me quick, come on and rock and roll for old___ Saint Nick. An-oth-er

CHORUS

Rock and Roll___ Christ - mas, an-oth-er Christ-mas Rock and Roll,___
Rock and Roll___ Christ - mas, an-oth-er Christ-mas Rock and Roll,___
(as chorus 1)

Backing Vocals

Shoo bee doo bee doo bee dap bap bap shoo bee doo bee doo bee dap bap bap

pres - ents hang - ing from the tree,_ you'll nev-er guess what you got from me._ An-oth-er
all dressed up, so here to go,_ do I hear sleigh bells in the snow? An-oth-er

oooh_____ doo waaah___ dap bap

Rock and Roll___ Christ - mas, an-oth-er Christ-mas Rock and Roll,___ we
Rock and Roll___ Christ - mas, an-oth-er Christ-mas Rock and Roll,___ to -

shoo bee doo bee doo bee dap bap bap shoo bee doo bee doo bee dap bap bap

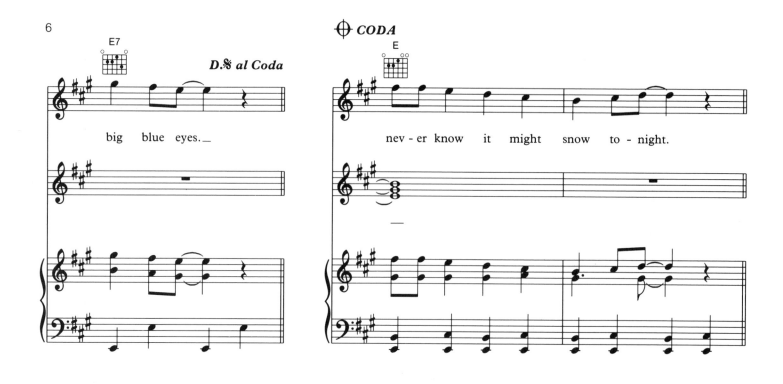

big blue eyes.___

nev - er know it might snow to - night.

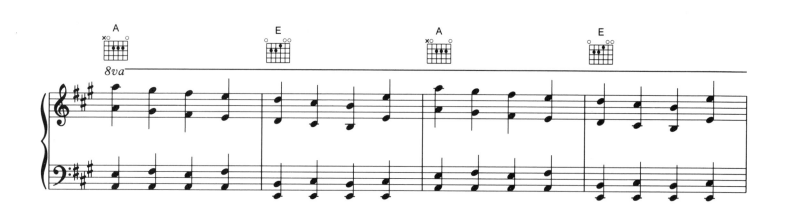

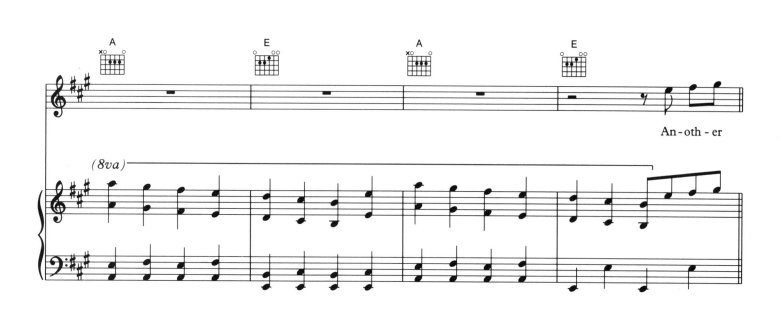

An - oth - er

-night old San - ta nev - er, nev - er stops, he bops a - bove the

bet - ter hold each oth - er tight,___ you nev - er know it might

oooh _____ doo waaah ___

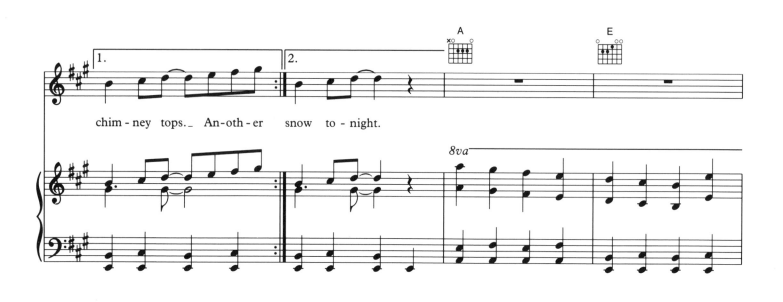

1.

2.

chim - ney tops.___ An - oth - er snow to - night.

A Winter's Tale

Words and Music by
Tim Rice and Mike Batt

Away In A Manger

Words Traditional
Music by William J Kirkpatrick

CD1

3. Be near me Lord Jesus
   I ask thee to stay
   Close by me forever
   And love me, I pray
   Bless all the dear children
   In thy tender care
   And fit us for heaven
   To live with thee there.

Christmas Alphabet

Words and Music by
Buddy Kaye and Jules Loman

CD1

The Christmas Song
(Chestnuts Roasting On An Open Fire)

Words and Music by
Mel Torme and Robert Wells

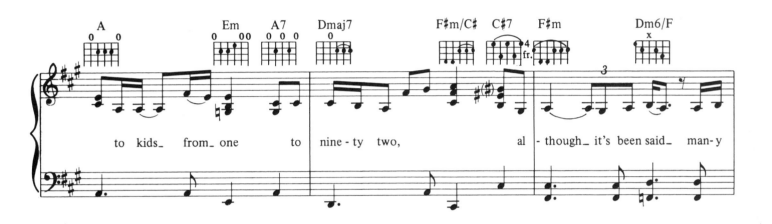

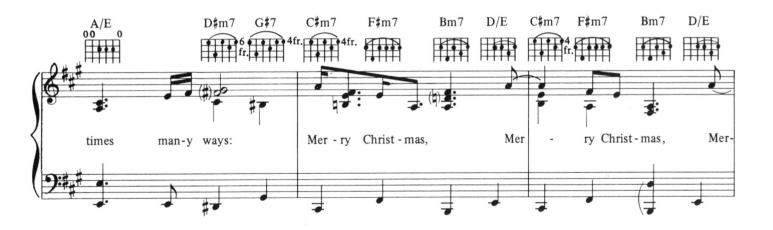

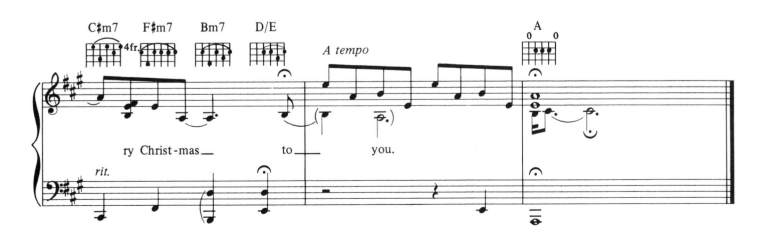

Ding! Dong! Merrily On High

CD1

Words by George Woodward and Charles Wood
Music Traditional

3. Pray you, dutifully prime
   Your matin chime, you ringers
   May you beautifully rhyme
   Your evetime song, you singers.

   Gloria, hosanna in excelsis
   Gloria, hosanna in excelsis!

The Fairytale Of New York

Words and Music by
Shane Mac-Gowan and Jem Finer

CD1

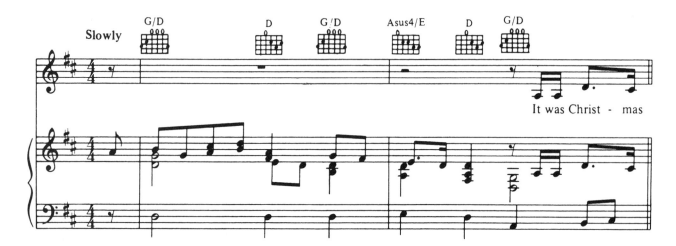

It was Christ - mas

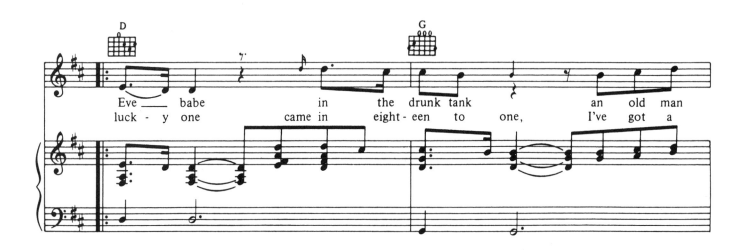

Eve ___ babe
luck - y one

in   the drunk tank
came in   eight-een to one,

an old man
I've got a

said to me,
feel - ing

won't see an - oth - er one.
this year's for me and you.

And then he
So hap - py

25

26

boys of the N. Y. P. D. Choir still sing-ing 'Gal - way Bay' and the

bells were ring - ing out on Christ-mas Day.)

(To Fade)

Frosty The Snowman

Words and Music by
Steve Nelson and Jack Rollins

Fros - ty the snow - man was a jol - ly hap - py soul,___ with a

Fros - ty the snow - man knew the sun was hot that day,___ so he

corn cob pipe and a but - ton nose___ and two eyes made out of

said "Let's run and we'll have some fun___ now be - fore I melt a -

coal. Fros — — ty the snow - man is a fair — y tale they say,
way." Down to the vil - lage with a broom - stick in his hand,

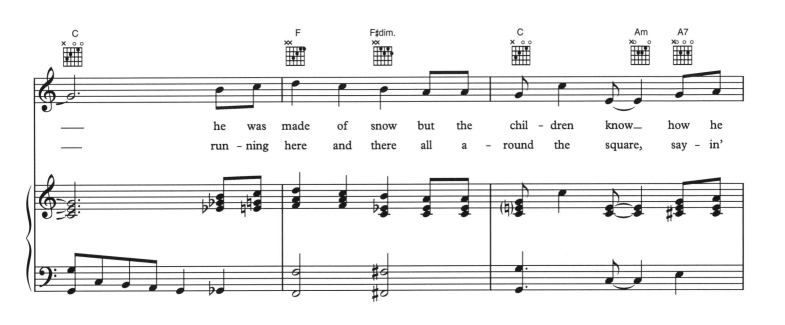

—— he was made of snow but the chil - dren know— how he
—— run - ning here and there all a - round the square, say - in'

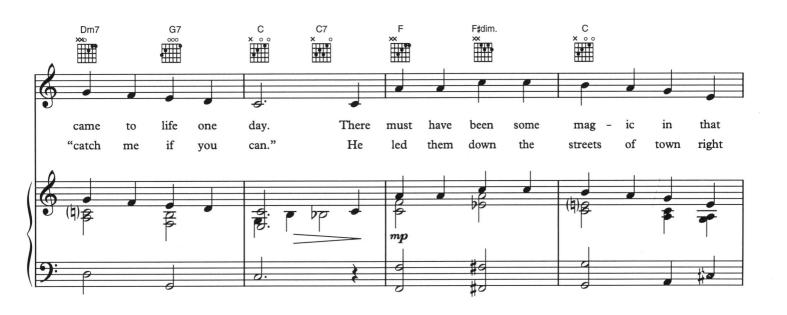

came to life one day. There must have been some mag - ic in that
"catch me if you can." He led them down the streets of town right

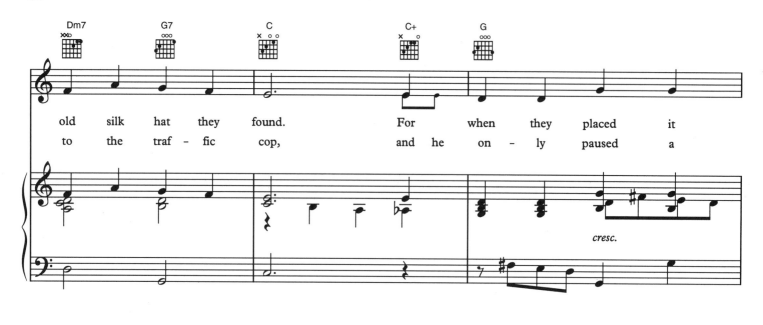

old silk hat they found. For when they placed it
to the traf-fic cop, and he on - ly paused a

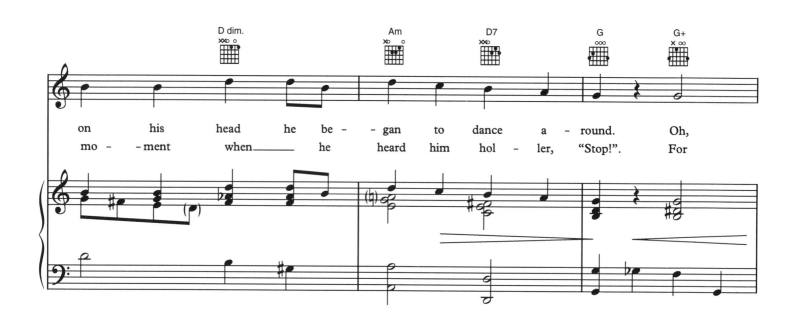

on his head he be - gan to dance a - round. Oh,
mo - -ment when_____ he heard him hol - ler, "Stop!". For

Fros - - ty the snow - man was a - live as he could be_____ and the
Fros - - ty the snow - man had to hur - ry on his way_____ but he

chil - dren say he could laugh and play_ just the same as you and me.
waved good - bye say - in', "Don't you cry,_ I'll be back a - gain some day."

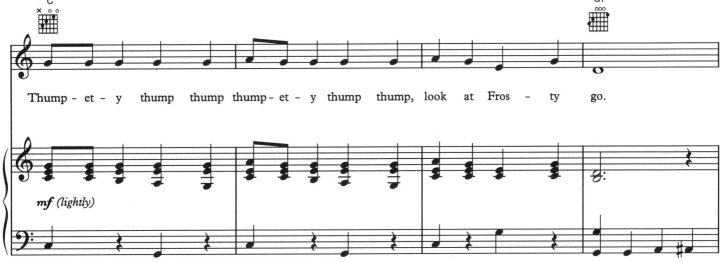

Thump - et - y thump thump thump - et - y thump thump, look at Fros - ty go.

mf (lightly)

Thump - et - y thump thump thump - et - y thump thump, o - ver the hills of snow.

f   sfz

Hark! The Herald Angels Sing

Words by Charles Wesley
Music by Felix Mendelssohn

CD1

1. Hark! The her-ald an-gels sing "Glo-ry to the new-born King!
2. Christ, by high-est heav'n a-dored, Christ, the ev-er-last-ing Lord.

Peace on earth and mer-cy mild, God and sin-ners re-con-ciled."
Late in time be-hold him come, off-spring of a vir-gin's womb.

3. Hail, the heaven-born Prince of Peace!
Hail, the Sun of Righteousness!
Light and life to all he brings
Risen with his healing wings
Mild He lays His glory by
Born that man no more may die
Born to raise the sons of earth
Born to give them second birth.

Hark! The herald angels sing
"Glory to the new-born king."

Have Yourself A Merry Little Christmas

Words and Music by
Hugh Martin and Ralph Blane

Slowly (in strict time)

CHORUS

Jingle Bells

Traditional

Allegro Moderato

Joy To The World

Words by Isaac Watts
Music by G F Handel

CD1

heaven and na - ture — sing, and — heaven and na - ture — sing, and —
- peat the sound - ing — joy, re - peat the sound - ing — joy, re -

heaven, — and heaven — and na - ture sing!
- peat, — re - peat — the sound - ing joy.

3. He rules the world with truth and grace
   And makes the nations prove
   The glories of his righteousness
   The wonders of his love
   The wonders of his love
   The wonders, wonders of his love.

Last Christmas

Words and Music by George Michael

The Little Boy That Santa Claus Forgot

CD1

Words and Music by Michael Carr,
Tommie Connor and Jimmy Leach

Slowly with feeling

Christ-mas comes but once a year for ev - 'ry girl and boy, the laugh-ter and the joy they

find in each new toy. I'll tell you of a lit - tle boy who

Let It Snow! Let It Snow! Let It Snow!

Words by Sammy Cahn
Music by Jule Styne

CD1

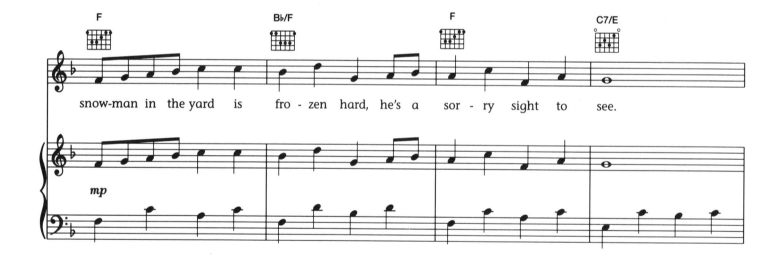

snow-man in the yard is fro-zen hard, he's a sor-ry sight to see.

If he had a brain he'd com-plain, bet he wish-es he were me. Oh the

so,   let   it snow, let   it snow, let   it snow.   Oh   the snow.

The snowman in the yard is frozen hard,
He's a sorry sight to see.
If he had a brain he'd complain,
Bet he wishes he were me.

Oh the weather outside is frightful.
But the fire is so delightful,
And since we've no place to go,
Let it snow, let it snow, let it snow.

It doesn't show signs of stopping,
And I brought some corn for popping,
The lights are turned way down low,
Let it snow, let it snow, let it snow.

When we finally kiss goodnight,
How I'll hate going out in the storm,
But if you really hold me tight,
All the way home I'll be warm.

The fire is slowly dying,
And my dear we're still goodbyeing,
But as long as you love me so,
Let it snow, let it snow, let it snow.

Little Donkey

Words and Music by Eric Boswell

Merry Christmas Everyone

Words and Music by Bob Heatlie

The Little Drummer Boy

CD2

Words and Music by Harry Simeone,
Henry Onorati and Katherine K Davis

O, Little Town Of Bethlehem

Words by Phillips Brooks
Music Traditional

in thy dark streets shi - neth the ev - er - last - ing light. The
Christ is born of Ma - ry, and gath - ered all a - bove. While

hopes and fears of all the years are met in thee to - night.
mor - tals sleep, the an - gels keep their watch of wond - 'ring love.

3. How silently, how silently
   The wondrous gift is given!
   So God imparts to human hearts
   The blessing of his heaven
   No ear may hear His coming
   But in this world of sin
   Where meek souls will receive Him still
   The dear Christ enters in.

4. Where children pure and happy
   Pray to the blessèd child
   Where misery cries out to thee
   Son of mother mild
   Where charity stands watching
   And faith holds wide the door
   The dark night wakes, the glory breaks
   And Christmas comes once more.

5. O holy child of Bethlehem!
   Descend to us, we pray
   Cast out our sin, and enter in
   Be born in us today
   We hear the Christmas angels
   The great glad tidings tell
   O come to us abide with us
   Our Lord Emmanuel.

Rockin' Around The Christmas Tree

Words and Music by Johnny Marks

Christ-mas tree, let the Christ-mas spir-it ring.— Lat-er we'll have some pun-kin pie— and we'll

do some car-ol-ing. You will get a sen-ti-men-tal feel-ing when you

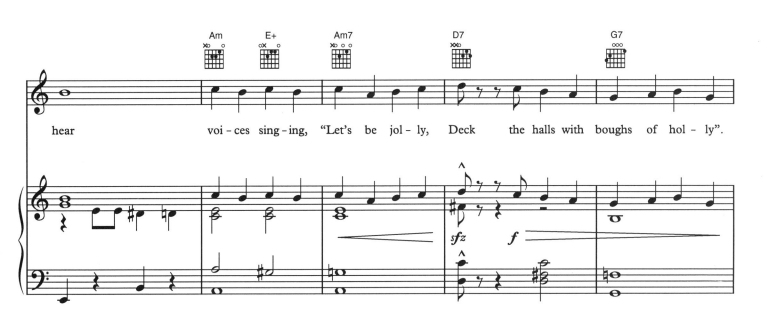

hear voi-ces sing-ing, "Let's be jol-ly, Deck the halls with boughs of hol-ly".

Rudolph The Red-Nosed Reindeer

CD2

Words and Music by Johnny Marks

Silent Night

Traditional

Si - lent night! Ho - ly night!
Si - lent night! Ho - ly night!

All is calm, all is bright.
Shep - herds quake at the sight!

Round yon Vir - gin Moth - er and Child!
Glo - ries stream from Hea - ven a - far,

Santa Claus Is Comin' To Town

Words by Haven Gillespie
Music by J Fred Coots

Track 8
CD2

Moderately

just came back from a love - ly trip a - long the Mil - ky Way,
San - ta is a ___ bu - sy man, he has no time to play,

I stopped off at the North Pole to spend a ho - li - day. ___ I
he's got mil - lions of stock - ings to fill on Christ - mas Day. ___ You'd

The First Nowell

Traditional

3. At Bethlehem they entered in
   On bended knee they worshipped him
   They offered there in his presence
   Their gold and myrrh and frankincense.

   Nowell, nowell, nowell, nowell
   Born is the king of Israel!

4. Then let us all with one accord
   Sing praises to our heavenly Lord
   For Christ has our salvation wrought
   And with his blood our life has bought.

   Nowell, nowell, nowell, nowell
   Born is the king of Israel!

The Holly And The Ivy

Traditional

CD2

1. The hol - ly and the i - vy, when they are both full grown, of___
2. The hol - ly bears a blos - som as white as a - ny flow'r, and___

all the trees that are in the wood, the___ hol - ly bears the crown.}
Ma - ry bore sweet___ Je - sus Christ to___ be our sweet sav - iour.} Oh, the

ris - ing   of   the   sun_____   and   the   run - ning   of   the   deer,   the__

play - ing   of   the   mer - ry   or - gan,   sweet   sing - ing   in   the   choir.

3. The holly bears a berry
   As red as any blood
   And Mary bore sweet Jesus Christ
   To do poor sinners good.

   The rising of the sun
   And the running of the deer
   The playing of the merry organ
   Sweet singing in the choir.

4. The holly bears a prickle
   As sharp as any thorn
   And Mary bore sweet Jesus Christ
   On Christmas Day in the morn.

   The rising of the sun
   And the running of the deer
   The playing of the merry organ
   Sweet singing in the choir.

5. The holly bears a bark
   As bitter as any gall
   And Mary bore sweet Jesus Christ
   For to redeem us all.

   The rising of the sun
   And the running of the deer
   The playing of the merry organ
   Sweet singing in the choir.

Sleigh Ride

Words by Mitchell Parish
Music by Leroy Anderson

Just hear those sleigh bells jin-gle-ing, ring-ting-tin-gle-ing too,

— come on, it's love-ly weath-er for a sleigh ride to-geth-er with you.

— Out-side the snow is fall-ing and friends are call-ing "Yoo hoo,"

Gid-dy-yap, gid-dy-yap, gid-dy-yap, it's grand, just hold-ing your

hand, we're glid-ing a-long with a song of a win-ter-y fair-y

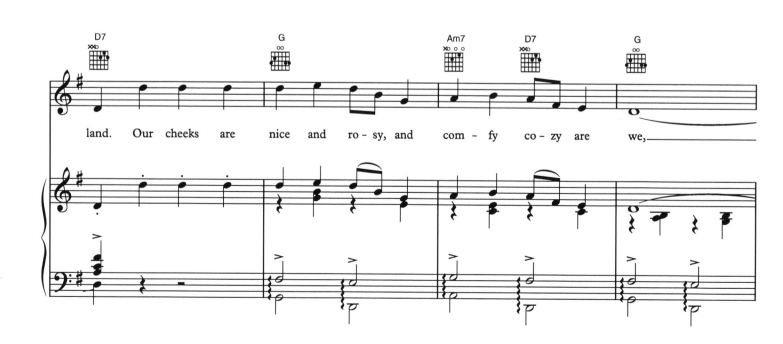

land. Our cheeks are nice and ro-sy, and com-fy co-zy are we,

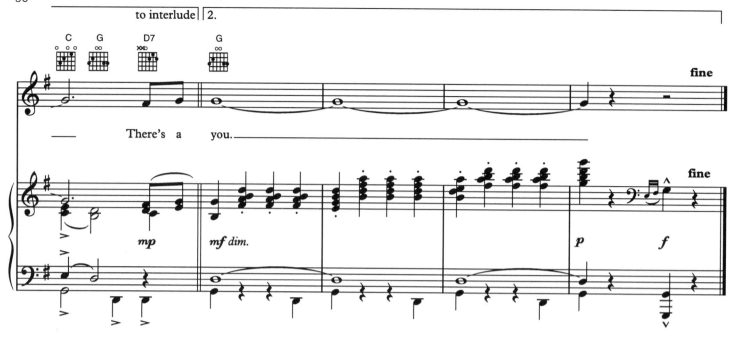

to interlude | 2.

C G D7 G

fine

fine

There's a you.

mp mf dim. p f

Interlude

Gmaj7

birth - day par - ty at the home of Farm - - - er Gray, it - 'll

mp f mp

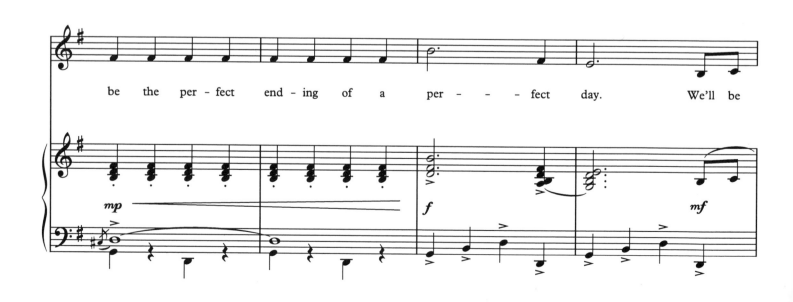

be the per - fect end - ing of a per - - - fect day. We'll be

mp f mf

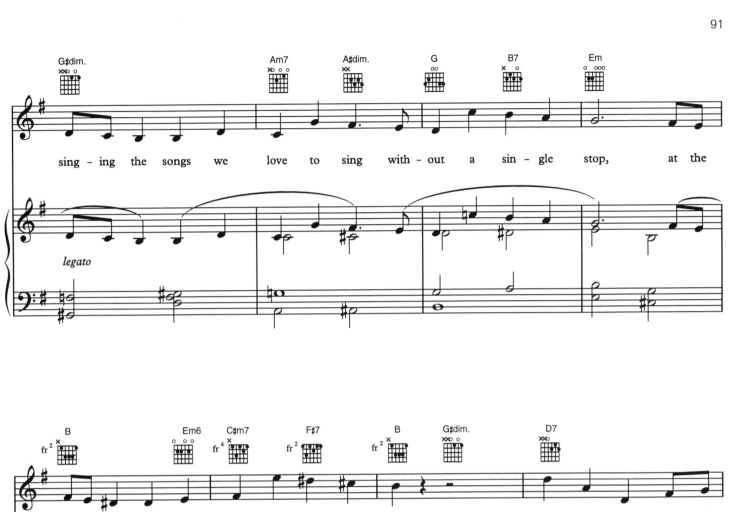

sing - ing the songs we love to sing with - out a sin - gle stop, at the

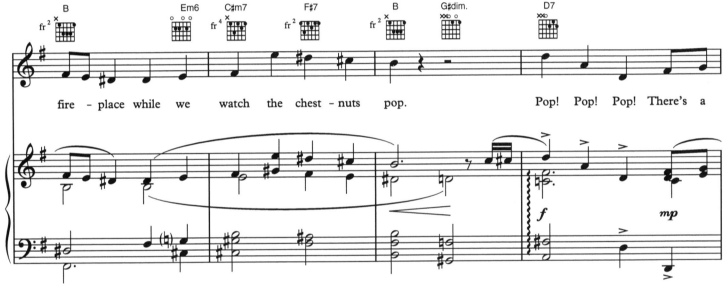

fire - place while we watch the chest - nuts pop. Pop! Pop! Pop! There's a

hap - py feel - ing noth - ing in the world can buy, when they

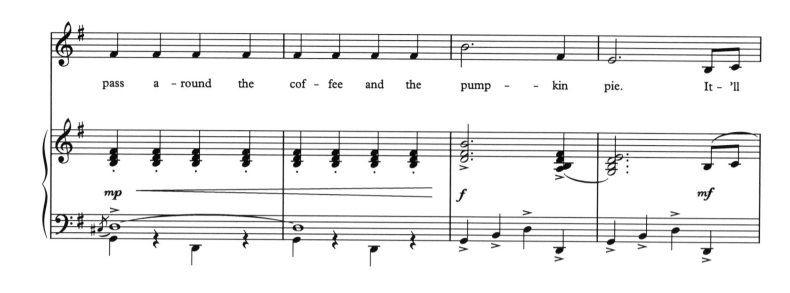

pass a - round the cof - fee and the pump - - kin pie. It - 'll

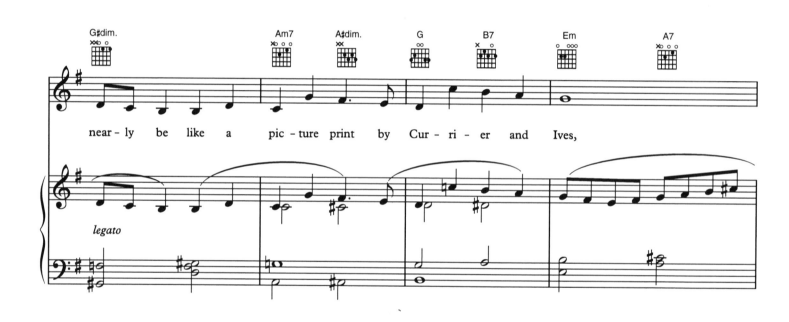

near - ly be like a pic - ture print by Cur - ri - er and Ives,

legato

these won - der - ful things are the things we re - mem - ber all thru our lives! Just hear those

D. %. al fine

The Twelve Days Of Christmas

Traditional

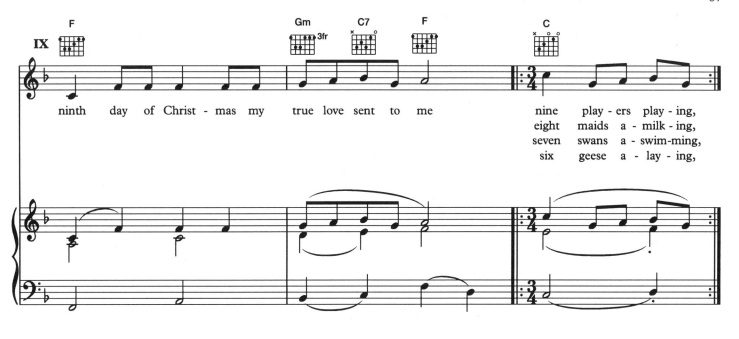

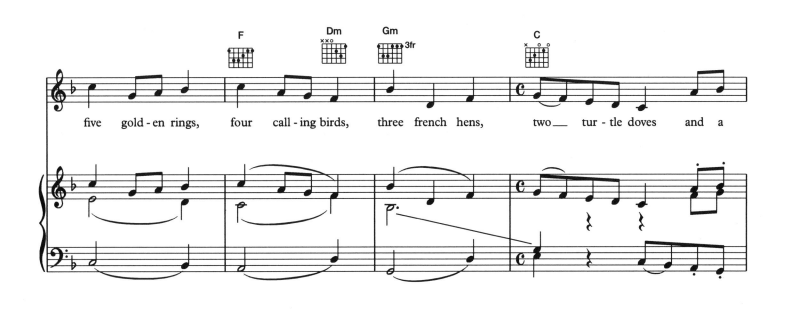

We Wish You A Merry Christmas

Traditional

CD2

wish you a Mer - ry Christ - mas and a Hap - py New Year!

2. Now bring us some figgy pudding
   Now bring us some figgy pudding
   Now bring us some figgy pudding
   And bring some out here.
   Good tidings, *etc.*

3. For we all like figgy pudding
   For we all like figgy pudding
   For we all like figgy pudding
   So bring some out here.
   Good tidings, *etc.*

4. And we won't go until we've got some
   And we won't go until we've got some
   And we won't go until we've got some
   So bring some out here.
   Good tidings, *etc.*

Winter Wonderland

Words by Dick Smith
Music by Felix Bernard

Moderato

O - ver the ground lies a man - tle of white, a hea - ven of dia - monds shine down thro' the night,__ two hearts are thrill - in' in spite of the chill__ in the wea - ther.

Francis Day & Hunter Ltd, London WC2H 0QY and Redwood Music Ltd, London NW1 8BD

When A Child Is Born

Slowly, with feeling

Words by Fred Jay
Music by Zacar

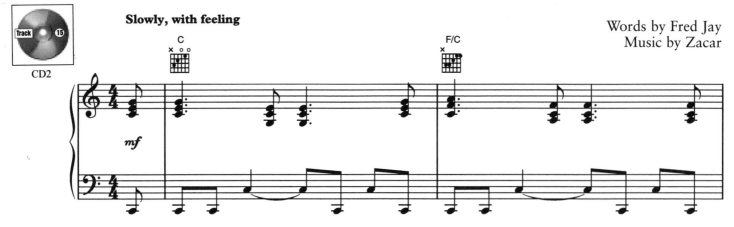

A ray of hope flick-ers in the
wish sails the se-ven

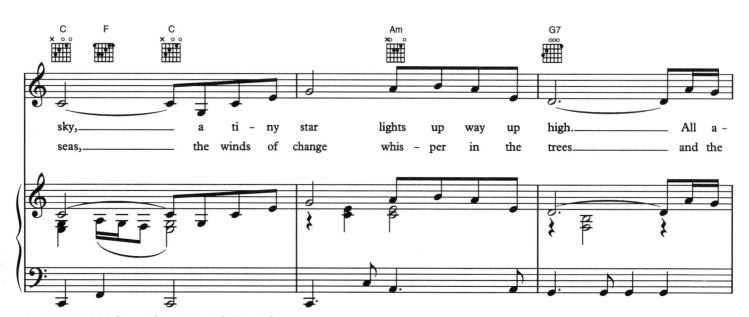

sky,_____ a ti-ny star lights up way up high._____ All a-
seas,_____ the winds of change whis-per in the trees_____ and the

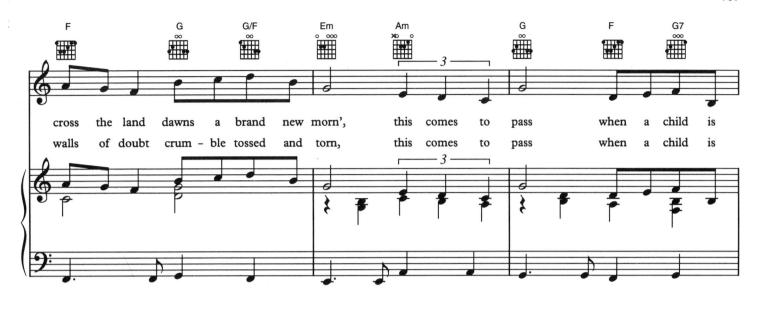

cross the land dawns a brand new morn', this comes to pass when a child is
walls of doubt crum - ble tossed and torn, this comes to pass when a child is

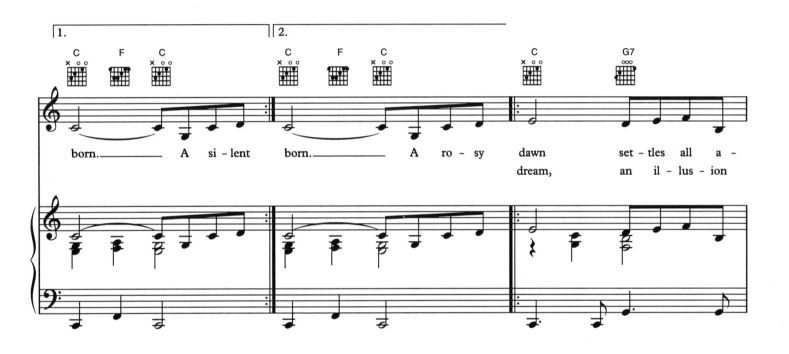

born._____ A si - lent born._____ A ro - sy dawn set - tles all a -
dream, an il - lus - ion

round,_____ you got the feel you're on sol - id ground._____ For a
now,_____ it must come true some - time soon some - how._____ All a -

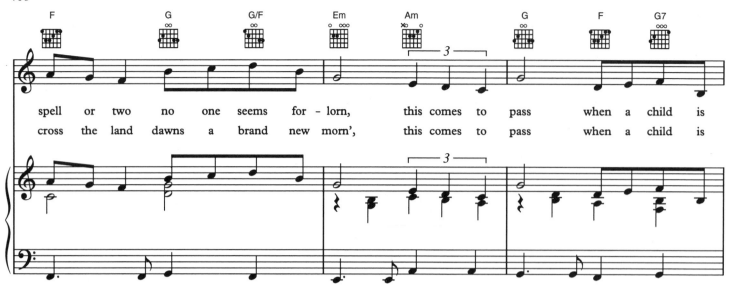

spell or two no one seems for - lorn, this comes to pass when a child is
cross the land dawns a brand new morn', this comes to pass when a child is

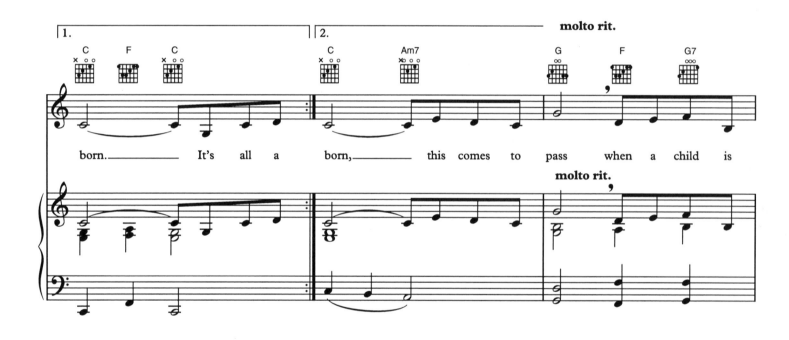

born._____ It's all a born,_____ this comes to pass when a child is

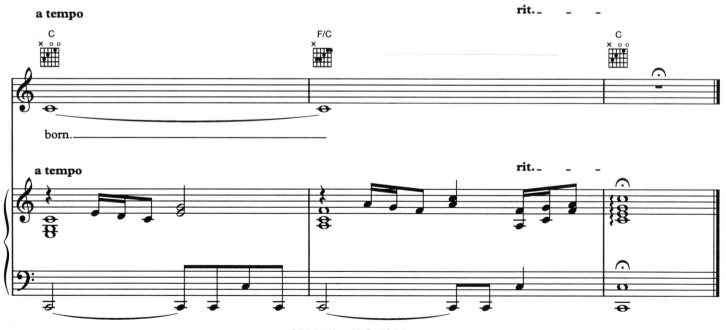

born._____